LOOK INSIDE
CROSS-SECTIONS
CARS

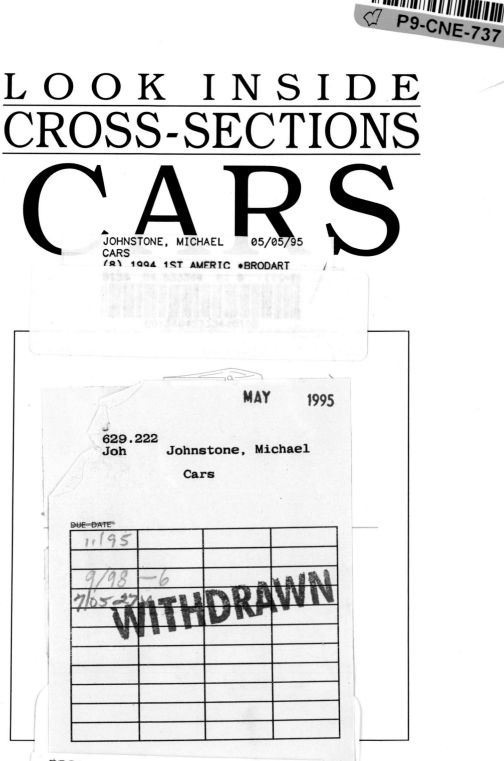

LOOK INSIDE
CROSS-SECTIONS
CARS

ILLUSTRATED BY
ALAN AUSTIN

WRITTEN BY
MICHAEL JOHNSTONE

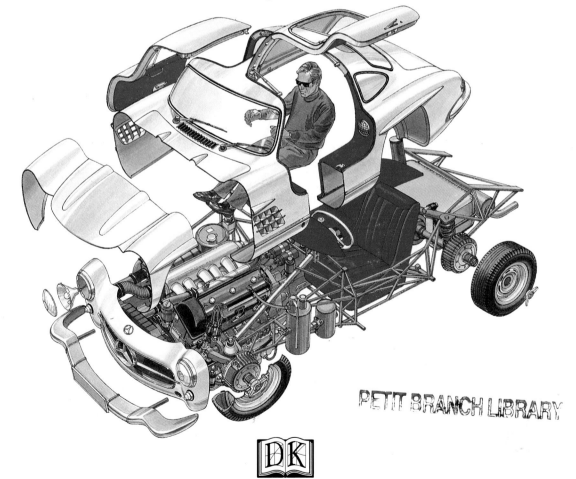

DK

DORLING KINDERSLEY
LONDON • NEW YORK • STUTTGART

A DORLING KINDERSLEY BOOK

Art Editor Dorian Spencer Davies
Designers Sharon Grant, Sara Hill
Senior Art Editor C. David Gillingwater
Project Editor Constance Novis
Senior Editor John C. Miles
U.S. Assistant Editor Camela Decaire
Production Louise Barratt
Consultant Jonathan Day
The National Motor Museum,
Beaulieu, England

First American edition, 1994
2 4 6 8 10 9 7 5 3 1
Published in the United States
by Dorling Kindersley Publishing, Inc.,
95 Madison Avenue, New York, New York 10016

Library of Congress Cataloging - in - Publication Data

Johnstone, Michael.
Cars / written by Michael Johnstone;
illustrated by Alan Austin. – 1st American ed.
p. cm. – (Look inside cross-sections)
Includes index.
ISBN 1-56458-681-2
1. Automobiles – Juvenile literature.
[1. Automobiles.]
I. Austin, Alan, ill.
II. Title. III. Series.
TL147. J645 1994
629. 222 – dc20   94 – 18481
                                    CIP
                                    AC

Reproduced by Dot Gradations, Essex
Printed and bound by Proost, Belgium

CONTENTS

FORD MODEL T

IN THE EARLY YEARS OF AUTOMOBILES, only the rich could afford a car. Henry Ford changed that. In 1903, he founded the Ford Motor Company and produced the Model A. It was based on the shape of a horse-drawn buggy, but with an engine under the seat! Five years later, the Model T appeared: it sold for $825. By 1927, when it went out of production, 5,007,033 "tin lizzies" had been produced and the price had fallen to $260. In 1913, Ford introduced a moving assembly line, operated by a windlass. By the end of that year, Ford workers could assemble a complete car in 93 minutes. Other car manufacturers took days, even weeks, to make their cars, which meant they were much more expensive.

"Any color they want ..."

Early Model Ts came in red, gray, and green. In 1914, the only paint that would dry quickly enough to keep up with the speed of the assembly line was black Japanese enamel. When Ford heard this, he said that anyone who wanted to buy a Model T could have it in any color they wanted – "as long as it's black!"

Stopping, reversing, and speeding

To stop the car, the driver pressed down the right-hand brake pedal. To put it in reverse, he put the car in neutral and then pressed down the middle pedal. The driver controlled the car's speed by pulling on a "throttle" handle.

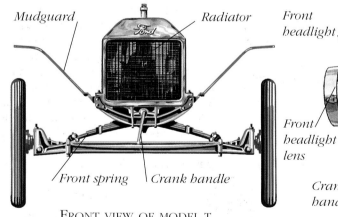

FRONT VIEW OF MODEL T

Mudguard · Radiator · Front spring · Crank handle

Getting started

Drivers of early Model Ts had to start them by cranking the engine. They fitted one end of a starting handle through a hole under the radiator leading into the engine. Then they turned the handle until the engine spluttered into life. If the ignition switch was in the wrong position, the starting handle would spring back violently when the engine started, leaving many inexperienced motorists with broken arms, wrists, or thumbs!

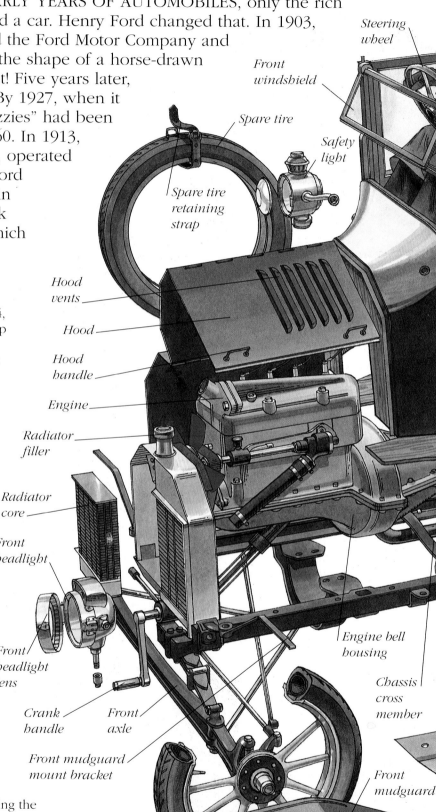

Steering wheel · Front windshield · Spare tire · Safety light · Spare tire retaining strap · Hood vents · Hood · Hood handle · Engine · Radiator filler · Radiator core · Front headlight · Front headlight lens · Crank handle · Front axle · Front mudguard mount bracket · Engine bell housing · Chassis cross member · Front mudguard

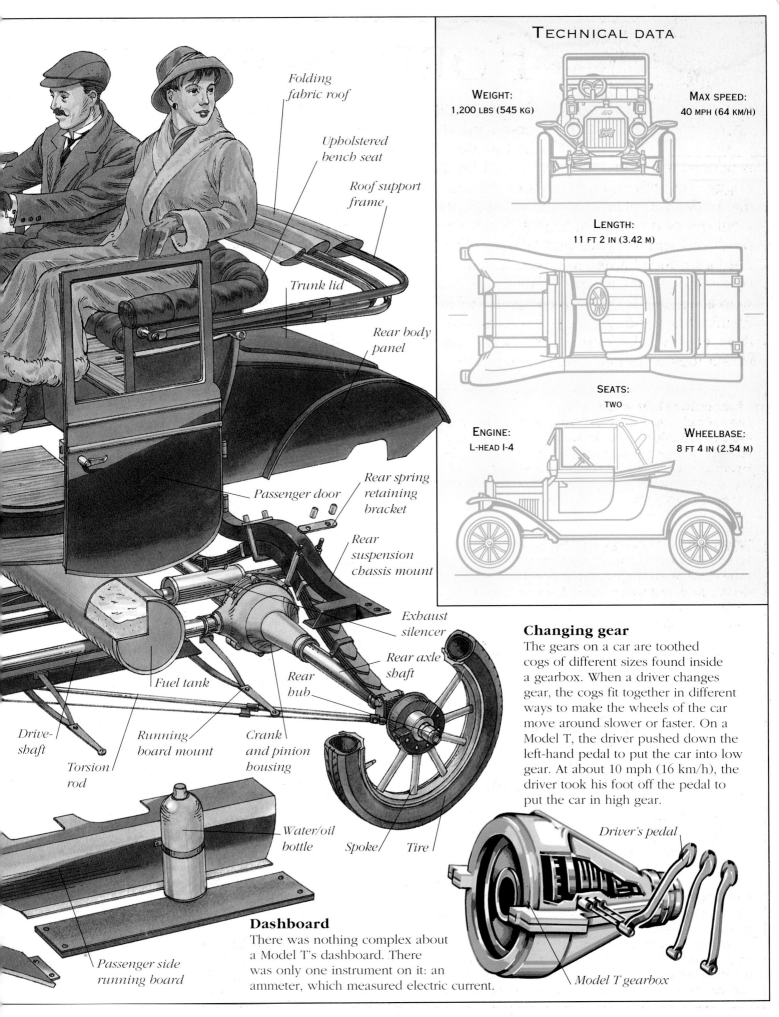

Folding fabric roof

Upholstered bench seat

Roof support frame

Trunk lid

Rear body panel

Passenger door

Rear spring retaining bracket

Rear suspension chassis mount

Exhaust silencer

Rear axle shaft

Fuel tank

Rear hub

Crank and pinion housing

Drive-shaft

Running board mount

Torsion rod

Water/oil bottle

Spoke

Tire

Passenger side running board

WEIGHT:
1,200 LBS (545 KG)

MAX SPEED:
40 MPH (64 KM/H)

LENGTH:
11 FT 2 IN (3.42 M)

SEATS:
TWO

ENGINE:
L-HEAD I-4

WHEELBASE:
8 FT 4 IN (2.54 M)

Changing gear

The gears on a car are toothed cogs of different sizes found inside a gearbox. When a driver changes gear, the cogs fit together in different ways to make the wheels of the car move around slower or faster. On a Model T, the driver pushed down the left-hand pedal to put the car into low gear. At about 10 mph (16 km/h), the driver took his foot off the pedal to put the car in high gear.

Driver's pedal

Model T gearbox

Dashboard

There was nothing complex about a Model T's dashboard. There was only one instrument on it: an ammeter, which measured electric current.

BENTLEY

EARLY IN THE DEVELOPMENT OF THE CAR, enthusiasts found a way of increasing the power of the engine. The device used to do this was called a supercharger. Superchargers, or "blowers," were first used in the mid-1920s. Bentley cars were first supercharged in 1928 when Sir Henry "Tim" Birkin, driving a standard Bentley, finished eighth in a race in Germany. He approached an engineer named Amherst Villiers to design the supercharger, and although only a handful of Bentley Blowers were built, they have become, in the eyes of many, the most sought-after cars in the world.

SUPERCHARGER DETAILS

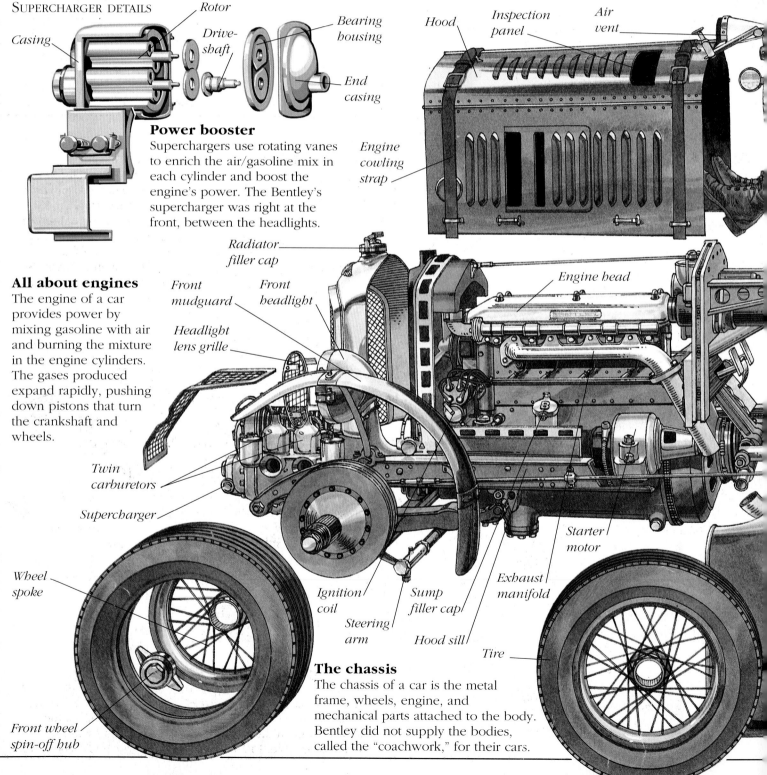

Casing
Rotor
Drive-shaft
Bearing housing
End casing

Power booster
Superchargers use rotating vanes to enrich the air/gasoline mix in each cylinder and boost the engine's power. The Bentley's supercharger was right at the front, between the headlights.

Hood
Inspection panel
Air vent

Engine cowling strap

Radiator filler cap

Engine head

All about engines
The engine of a car provides power by mixing gasoline with air and burning the mixture in the engine cylinders. The gases produced expand rapidly, pushing down pistons that turn the crankshaft and wheels.

Front mudguard
Front headlight

Headlight lens grille

Twin carburetors

Supercharger

Wheel spoke

Ignition coil

Steering arm

Sump filler cap

Hood sill

Exhaust manifold

Starter motor

Tire

Front wheel spin-off hub

The chassis
The chassis of a car is the metal frame, wheels, engine, and mechanical parts attached to the body. Bentley did not supply the bodies, called the "coachwork," for their cars.

The dashboard

The dashboard in the Blower was made of aluminum and housed more instruments than many aircraft of the day. There was no standard layout, but in most models the speedometer was just to the left of the steering wheel. The fuel gauge was alongside it to the left, just below the tachometer, which showed the driver how hard the engine was working by counting the revs.

Air screen

Racing goggles

Steering wheel

Driver's seat

Folding roof

TECHNICAL DATA

MAX SPEED:
120 MPH (193 KM/H)

WHEELBASE:
10 FT 10 IN (3.30 M)

ENGINE:
4-CYLINDER NONDETACHABLE HEAD

WEIGHT:
2,850 LBS (1,451 KG) WITHOUT COACHWORK

Gear-shift

Hand brake

Cockpit dash-board

Fuel tank filler

On the road

The rules of the Le Mans, the 24-hour race held every year in France, said that at least 50 examples of any model in the competition must be offered for sale to the public. Bentley therefore made 50 production cars as well as the racing models.

Rear mesh covering

Tail-light

Fuel tank

Rear suspension damper

Rear axle spline

Driveshaft coupling

Floor panel

Link arm

Linkage rod

Rear coach spring

Rear differential

Passenger door

Rear brake drum

"Corrupt"

Walter O. Bentley, the man who founded the company, did not want his cars supercharged. "To supercharge a Bentley," he said, "is to corrupt its performance." Even before the Blower was on the road, the Bentley company was in financial trouble. In 1931, it was taken over by Rolls-Royce.

9

CITROEN

IN 1932, FRENCH CARMAKER André Citroën announced that he would build a strong, light car with some very innovative features. Within eighteen months, he was true to his word and the first *Traction Avant*, the "A-series" 7cv, appeared on the road. His great achievement was to produce a car with up-to-the-minute engineering at a price that ordinary people could afford. He died almost bankrupt in 1935, but his *Traction Avant* stayed in production in various models until 1957. Even today there are still some on the road, cherished by their fortunate owners.

Pulling from the front

Citroën decided that his car would have front wheel drive, with which the car is pulled along by its front wheels as opposed to being pushed along by its rear ones. Hence the name *Traction Avant*, French for "pulling front."

Styled for ewe

Early Citroën advertising showed how, with its flat floor, the *Traction Avant* could be used to transport animals, such as sheep, in the back.

Keeping things level

Suspension systems keep a car's wheels on the road, no matter how bumpy, and protect passengers from being shaken too much. Early cars had simple springs to absorb the shock. The *Traction Avant* was fitted with bars called torsion bars, which acted as springs.

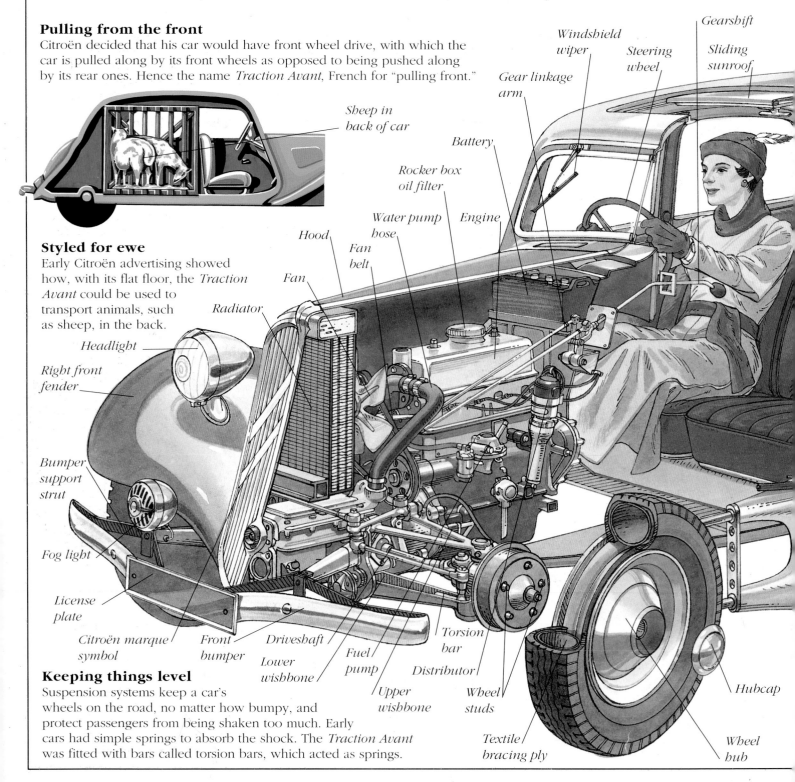

Sheep in back of car

Gearshift

Windshield wiper

Steering wheel

Sliding sunroof

Gear linkage arm

Battery

Rocker box oil filter

Water pump hose

Engine

Hood

Fan belt

Fan

Radiator

Headlight

Right front fender

Bumper support strut

Fog light

License plate

Citroën marque symbol

Front bumper

Driveshaft

Lower wishbone

Fuel pump

Upper wishbone

Torsion bar

Distributor

Wheel studs

Textile bracing ply

Hubcap

Wheel hub

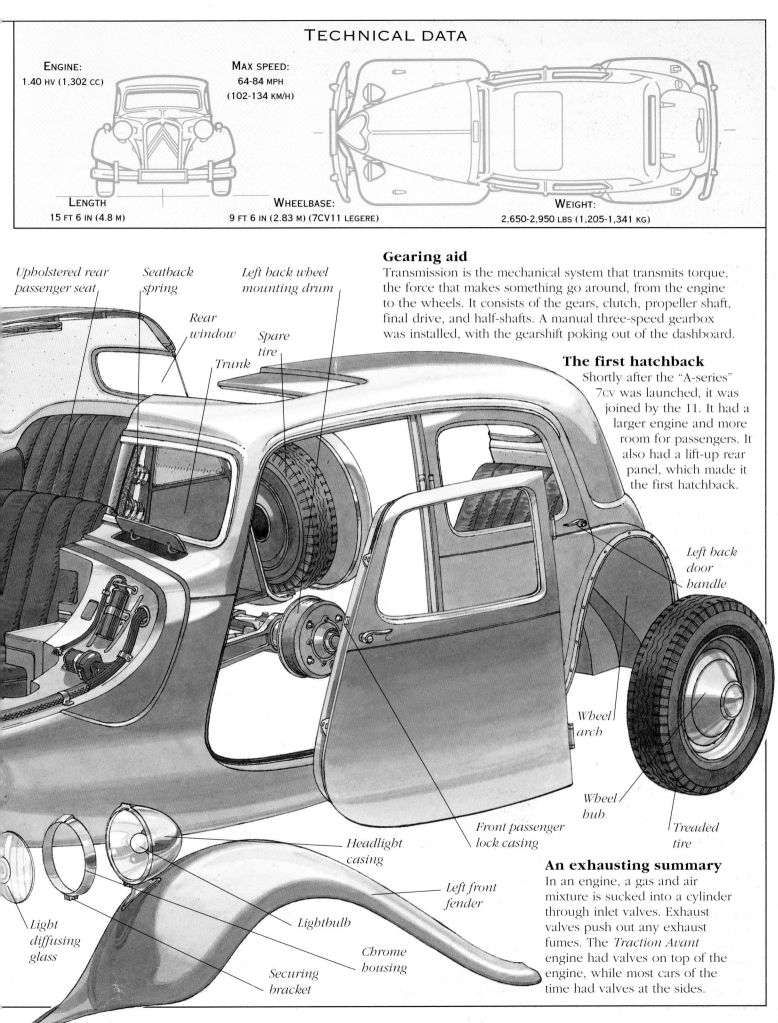

TECHNICAL DATA

ENGINE:
1.40 HV (1,302 CC)

MAX SPEED:
64-84 MPH
(102-134 KM/H)

LENGTH
15 FT 6 IN (4.8 M)

WHEELBASE:
9 FT 6 IN (2.83 M) (7CV11 LEGERE)

WEIGHT:
2,650-2,950 LBS (1,205-1,341 KG)

Upholstered rear passenger seat

Seatback spring

Left back wheel mounting drum

Rear window

Spare tire

Trunk

Left back door handle

Wheel arch

Wheel hub

Treaded tire

Headlight casing

Front passenger lock casing

Left front fender

Lightbulb

Chrome housing

Securing bracket

Light diffusing glass

Gearing aid

Transmission is the mechanical system that transmits torque, the force that makes something go around, from the engine to the wheels. It consists of the gears, clutch, propeller shaft, final drive, and half-shafts. A manual three-speed gearbox was installed, with the gearshift poking out of the dashboard.

The first hatchback

Shortly after the "A-series" 7cv was launched, it was joined by the 11. It had a larger engine and more room for passengers. It also had a lift-up rear panel, which made it the first hatchback.

An exhausting summary

In an engine, a gas and air mixture is sucked into a cylinder through inlet valves. Exhaust valves push out any exhaust fumes. The *Traction Avant* engine had valves on top of the engine, while most cars of the time had valves at the sides.

WILLYS JEEP

THE US ARMY USED the Jeep for everything in World War II. In the words of one expert, "it laid smoke screens and furnished hot water for shaving, served as a mobile command post, front line ambulance, field telephone station, fire engine, and snowplow ... delivered fresh socks and rations, towed artillery and airplanes, and its broad, flat hood was used as a map table, dining table, and an altar for religious services ..." No wonder the Jeep has been hailed as America's greatest contribution to modern warfare!

Back seat (foldable)

Spare wheel and tire

Collapsible roof framework

Rear wheel well

Rear damper

Four-wheel drive

Jeeps are four-wheel drive vehicles, which means that the engine can turn either the front wheels (which pull the car along) or the back wheels (which push it forward), or both. Four-wheel drive, combined with the Jeep's big engine, enabled the Jeep to get out of the trickiest situations.

Exhaust tailpipe

Leaf spring suspension

Rear wheel mounting hub

Differential housing

Collapsible roof tarpaulin

What's in a name

Prototypes had the letters GP (for general purpose) painted on their sides. Early models were given names such as "Bug," "Blitz Buggy," "Peep," "Midget," "Quack," and "Quad," but when one GI saw the letters GP, he ran them together and coined the name "Jeep." It stuck.

"What we want is ..."

American military authorities specified a vehicle able to ford water, drive up a 45-degree slope, and down a 35-degree one when they ordered the truck that became the Jeep.

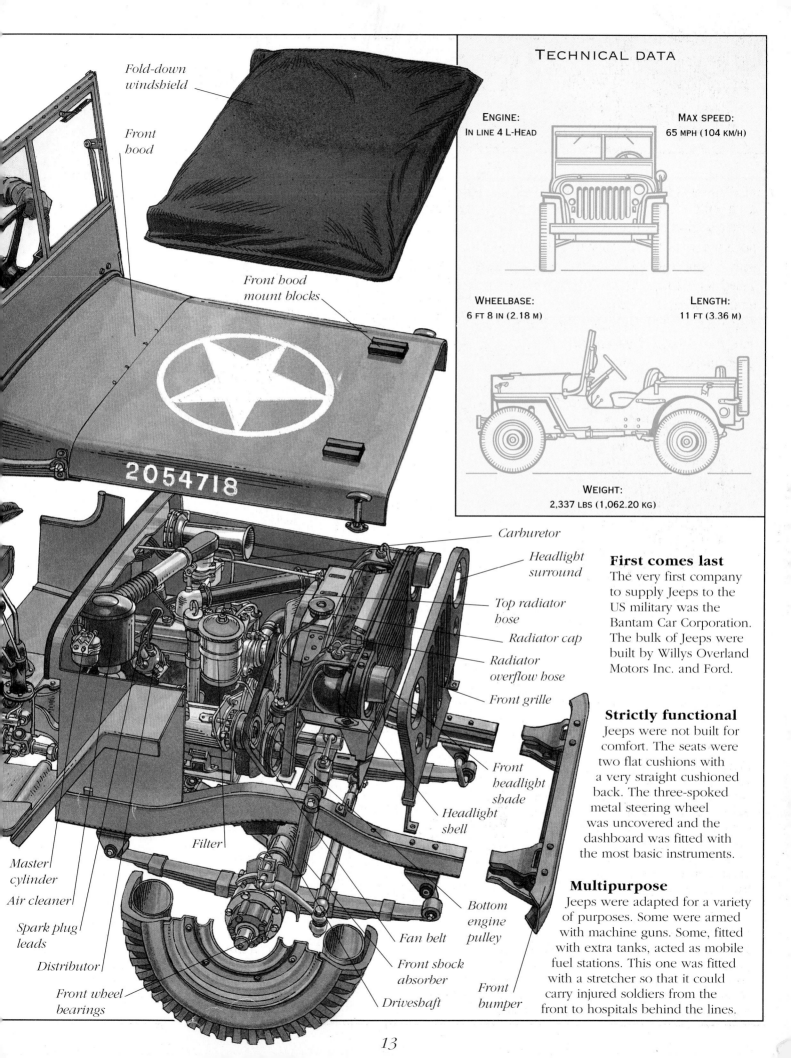

Fold-down windshield

Front hood

Front hood mount blocks

2054718

ENGINE:
IN LINE 4 L-HEAD

MAX SPEED:
65 MPH (104 KM/H)

WHEELBASE:
6 FT 8 IN (2.18 M)

LENGTH:
11 FT (3.36 M)

WEIGHT:
2,337 LBS (1,062.20 KG)

Carburetor

Headlight surround

Top radiator hose

Radiator cap

Radiator overflow hose

Front grille

Front headlight shade

Headlight shell

Master cylinder

Air cleaner

Spark plug leads

Distributor

Filter

Front wheel bearings

Front shock absorber

Driveshaft

Fan belt

Bottom engine pulley

Front bumper

First comes last

The very first company to supply Jeeps to the US military was the Bantam Car Corporation. The bulk of Jeeps were built by Willys Overland Motors Inc. and Ford.

Strictly functional

Jeeps were not built for comfort. The seats were two flat cushions with a very straight cushioned back. The three-spoked metal steering wheel was uncovered and the dashboard was fitted with the most basic instruments.

Multipurpose

Jeeps were adapted for a variety of purposes. Some were armed with machine guns. Some, fitted with extra tanks, acted as mobile fuel stations. This one was fitted with a stretcher so that it could carry injured soldiers from the front to hospitals behind the lines.

BEETLE

VOLKS = PEOPLE'S. *WAGEN* = CAR. HENCE *VOLKSWAGEN*. When this popular little car was launched, someone said it looked like a beetle, and the name stuck. It was developed because the German dictator, Adolf Hitler, decided that every German needed a car! He chose Ferdinand Porsche to design it. His directions were simple: design a small car that is cheap to run, able to carry a family of four or five, has a cruising speed of 62.5 mph (100 km/h), and is priced below 1,000 reichsmarks ($225 at today's value). A few handmade models were built for Nazi VIPs before the war, and between 1939 and 1945 only military VWs were built. Production at the Wolfsburg factory started in earnest after 1945 and the rest is history. Over 20 million Beetles were produced, and no other car has ever been in production for so long. The basic car shape was essentially the same throughout its life.

Sorry, you'll have to wait

Hitler decreed that people who wanted to buy a Volkswagen had to collect weekly savings stamps in advance. The war dashed any hopes that civilians may have had to own a VW. But when it was over, the company agreed to honor stamps that had been bought before 1939.

Back to front

The Volkswagen's engine is at the back, and its luggage space is at the front, the opposite of most cars. Inside the engine there are metal tubes called cylinders that contain combustion chambers, where fuel and air are burned. The Volkswagen engine has four cylinders.

Rear window

Air intake vents

Folding sunroof

Right rear seat

Seat structure

Driver's seat

Air cleaner

Ignition coil

License plate light

Generator

Rear light assembly

Oil filter

Over-rider

Tailpipe

Rear bumper

Right rear fender

Hubcap

Air-cooled flat four engine

Drive-shaft

Brake drum

Shock absorber

Trailing arm

Rear brake shoes

Torsion bar end

Heating hose

Wheel mounting hub

Volkswagen marque emblem

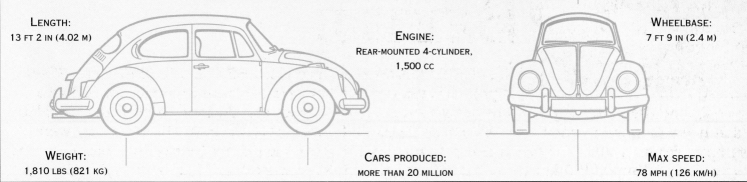

TECHNICAL DATA (1969 EXPORT MODEL)

LENGTH:
13 FT 2 IN (4.02 M)

ENGINE:
REAR-MOUNTED 4-CYLINDER,
1,500 CC

WHEELBASE:
7 FT 9 IN (2.4 M)

WEIGHT:
1,810 LBS (821 KG)

CARS PRODUCED:
MORE THAN 20 MILLION

MAX SPEED:
78 MPH (126 KM/H)

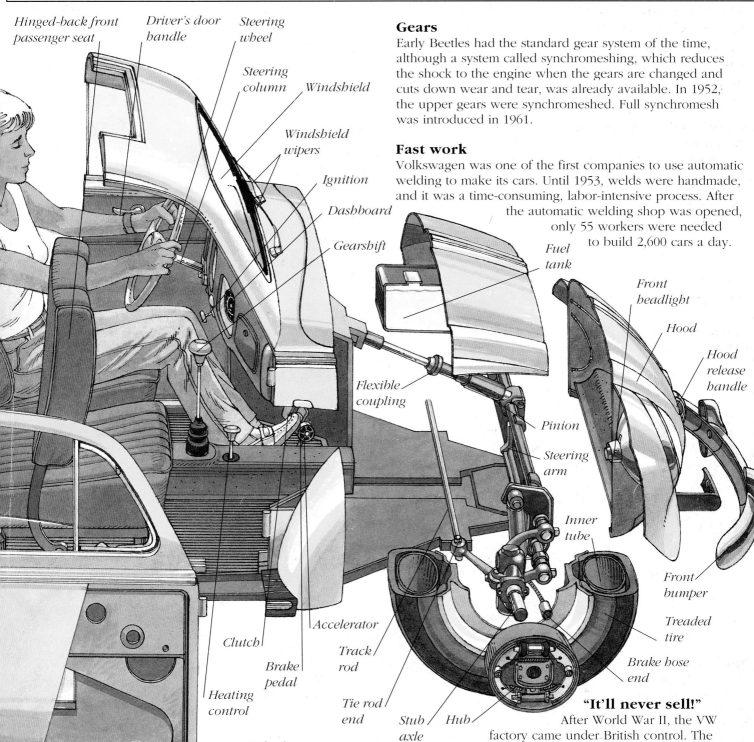

Gears

Early Beetles had the standard gear system of the time, although a system called synchromeshing, which reduces the shock to the engine when the gears are changed and cuts down wear and tear, was already available. In 1952, the upper gears were synchromeshed. Full synchromesh was introduced in 1961.

Fast work

Volkswagen was one of the first companies to use automatic welding to make its cars. Until 1953, welds were handmade, and it was a time-consuming, labor-intensive process. After the automatic welding shop was opened, only 55 workers were needed to build 2,600 cars a day.

"It'll never sell!"

After World War II, the VW factory came under British control. The British considered sponsoring production, but decided that the car had no future!

Labels: Hinged-back front passenger seat · Driver's door handle · Steering wheel · Steering column · Windshield · Windshield wipers · Ignition · Dashboard · Gearshift · Fuel tank · Front headlight · Hood · Hood release handle · Flexible coupling · Pinion · Steering arm · Inner tube · Front bumper · Treaded tire · Brake hose end · Clutch · Accelerator · Brake pedal · Track rod · Tie rod end · Stub axle · Hub · Heating control · Right door bottom hinge

GULLWING

IN 1952, THE CHAIRMAN of the German Daimler-Benz company wanted to show the world that his company meant business. The car to do it with was the new 300SL (Sports Light). SLs placed second and fourth in the 1952 Mille Miglia road race, and won both the Le Mans and the Mexican Carrera Panamericana in the same year. Mercedes-Benz had no plans to build production models until an American car importer ordered 1,000. The car was unveiled at the 1954 New York Auto Show, where it caused a sensation. Today, it still does!

Gullwing doors

The doors were hinged along the top and opened upward. This gave the car the nickname "Gullwing." If the driver parked too close to anything though, the doors could not be opened thanks to the huge arc they made swinging upward.

Gone, but not forgotten

In mid-1957, the Gullwing was replaced by the 300SL roadster with a frame designed for conventional doors. In all, 1,440 Gullwings and 1,858 roadsters were made.

Light or heavy

The racing sports model had a light metal alloy body, hence the designation SL, "Sports Light." It was not heavy enough for road models, which were built in much tougher steel, apart from the hood, doors, and trunk lid.

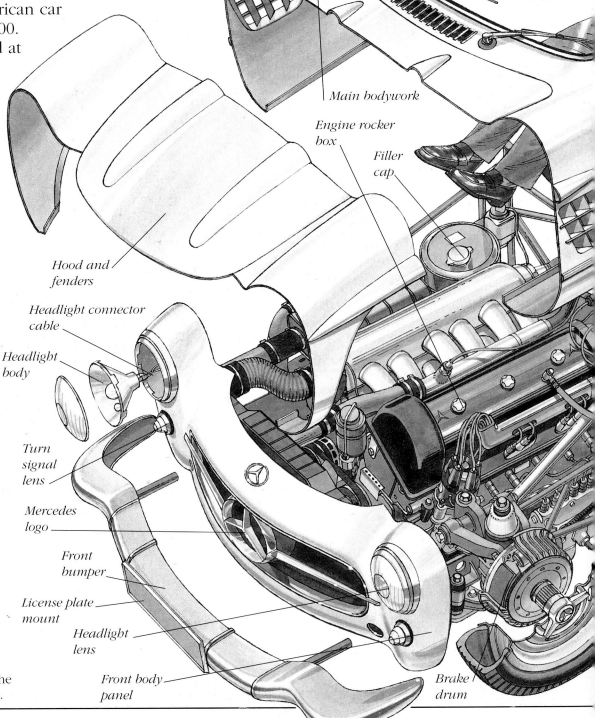

Windshield wiper

Main bodywork

Engine rocker box

Filler cap

Hood and fenders

Headlight connector cable

Headlight body

Turn signal lens

Mercedes logo

Front bumper

License plate mount

Headlight lens

Front body panel

Brake drum

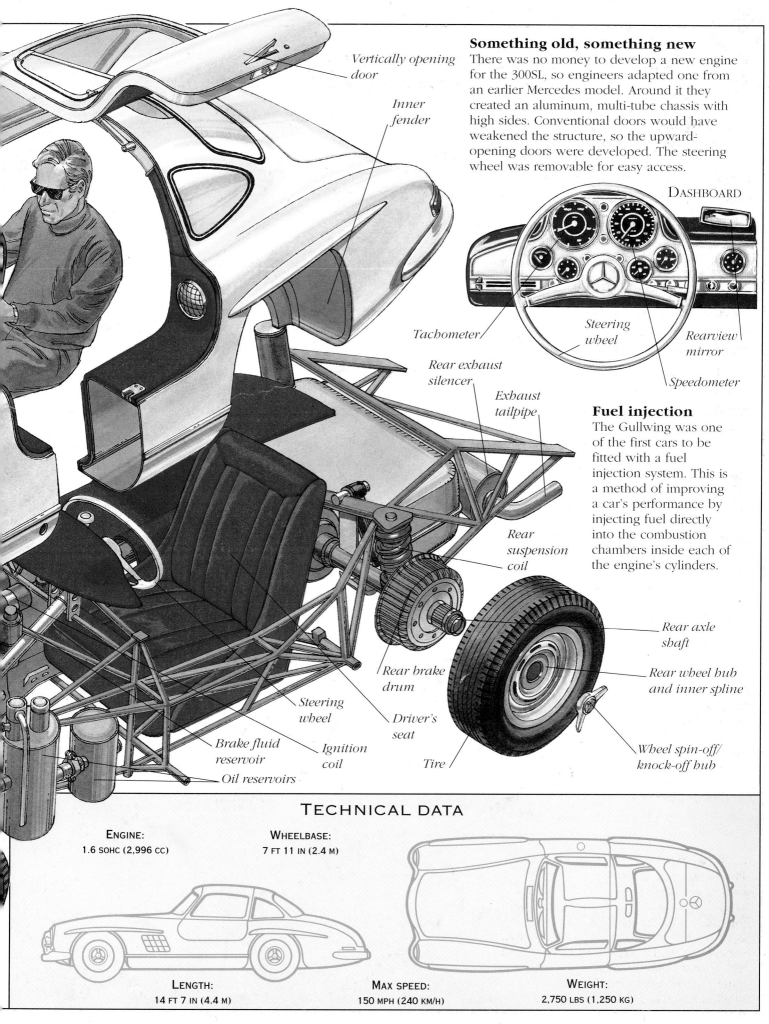

Vertically opening
door

Inner
fender

Something old, something new

There was no money to develop a new engine for the 300SL, so engineers adapted one from an earlier Mercedes model. Around it they created an aluminum, multi-tube chassis with high sides. Conventional doors would have weakened the structure, so the upward-opening doors were developed. The steering wheel was removable for easy access.

DASHBOARD

Tachometer

Steering
wheel

Rearview
mirror

Speedometer

Fuel injection

The Gullwing was one of the first cars to be fitted with a fuel injection system. This is a method of improving a car's performance by injecting fuel directly into the combustion chambers inside each of the engine's cylinders.

Rear exhaust
silencer

Exhaust
tailpipe

Rear
suspension
coil

Rear axle
shaft

Rear wheel hub
and inner spline

Rear brake
drum

Driver's
seat

Steering
wheel

Brake fluid
reservoir

Ignition
coil

Tire

Wheel spin-off/
knock-off hub

Oil reservoirs

TECHNICAL DATA

ENGINE:
1.6 SOHC (2,996 CC)

WHEELBASE:
7 FT 11 IN (2.4 M)

LENGTH:
14 FT 7 IN (4.4 M)

MAX SPEED:
150 MPH (240 KM/H)

WEIGHT:
2,750 LBS (1,250 KG)

CADILLAC

CADILLAC HAS BEEN MAKING CARS SINCE 1902, and millions of Americans have dreamed of owning one. To sit behind the wheel of a Cadillac is to tell the world that you are rich and successful – or have rich and successful parents! Cadillac has always taken the styles, taste, and mood of the day into account when designing its cars. In the 1950s, the cars were as bright and flashy as the rock'n'roll music that blared from their radios. Two of the greatest gas-guzzlers of these happy days were the 1957 Sedan de Ville and Coupe de Ville. They were about 18 ft (6 m) long, loaded with extravagant trim, from streamlined tail fins to a gleaming bumper and grille.

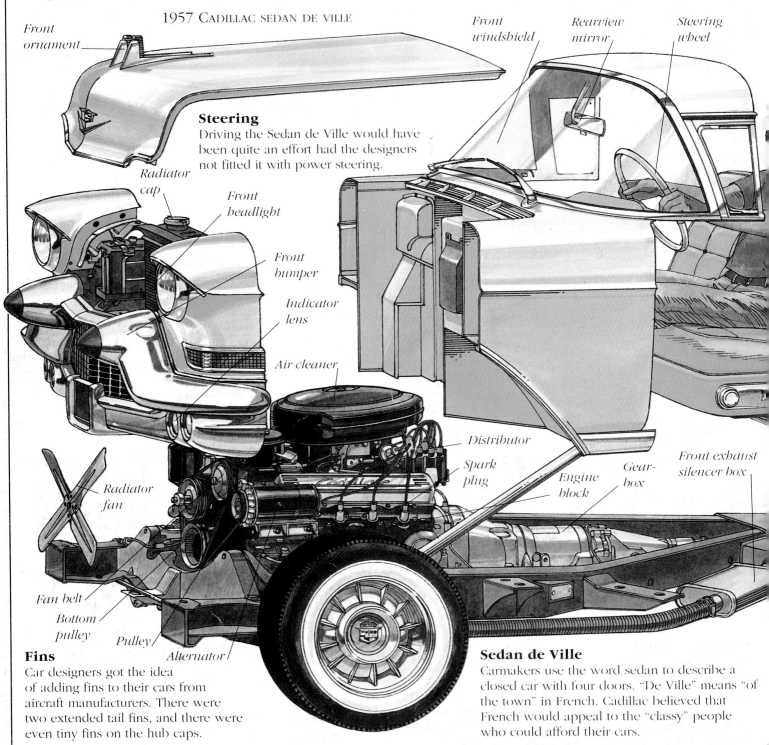

1957 CADILLAC SEDAN DE VILLE

Front ornament

Radiator cap

Front headlight

Front bumper

Indicator lens

Air cleaner

Radiator fan

Fan belt

Bottom pulley

Pulley

Alternator

Front windshield

Rearview mirror

Steering wheel

Distributor

Spark plug

Engine block

Gearbox

Front exhaust silencer box

Steering
Driving the Sedan de Ville would have been quite an effort had the designers not fitted it with power steering.

Fins
Car designers got the idea of adding fins to their cars from aircraft manufacturers. There were two extended tail fins, and there were even tiny fins on the hub caps.

Sedan de Ville
Carmakers use the word sedan to describe a closed car with four doors. "De Ville" means "of the town" in French. Cadillac believed that French would appeal to the "classy" people who could afford their cars.

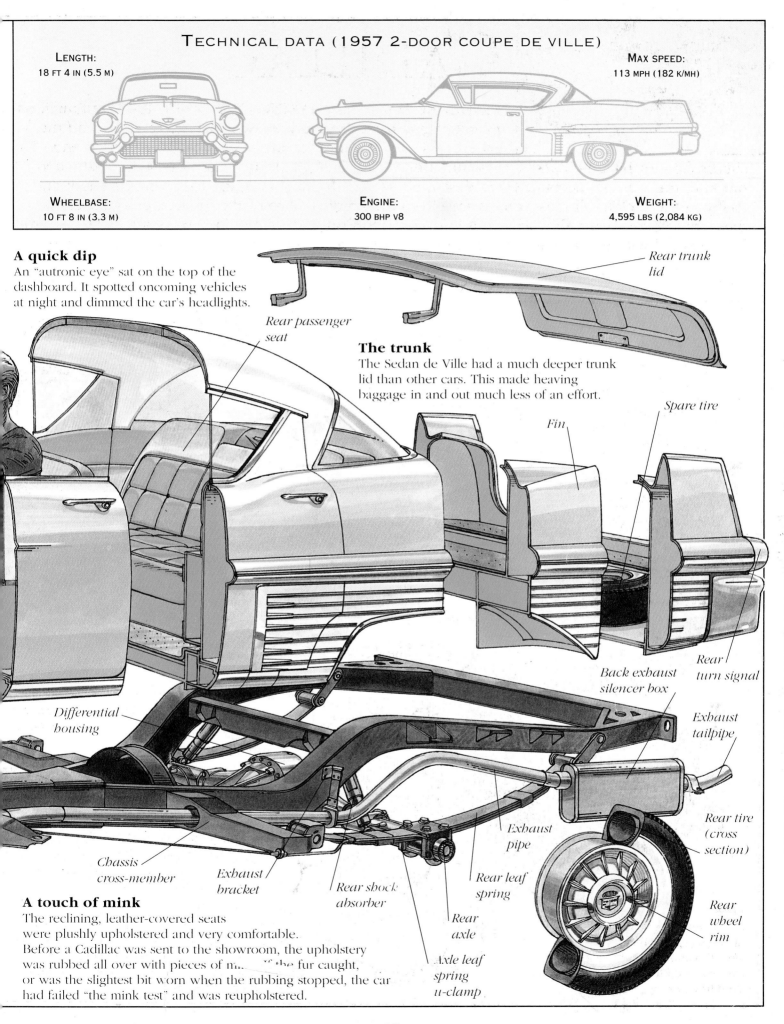

TECHNICAL DATA (1957 2-DOOR COUPE DE VILLE)

LENGTH:
18 FT 4 IN (5.5 M)

MAX SPEED:
113 MPH (182 K/MH)

WHEELBASE:
10 FT 8 IN (3.3 M)

ENGINE:
300 BHP V8

WEIGHT:
4,595 LBS (2,084 KG)

A quick dip
An "autronic eye" sat on the top of the dashboard. It spotted oncoming vehicles at night and dimmed the car's headlights.

Rear passenger seat

The trunk
The Sedan de Ville had a much deeper trunk lid than other cars. This made heaving baggage in and out much less of an effort.

Rear trunk lid

Spare tire

Fin

Rear turn signal

Back exhaust silencer box

Exhaust tailpipe

Differential housing

Rear tire (cross section)

Exhaust pipe

Rear leaf spring

Rear axle

Rear wheel rim

Chassis cross-member

Exhaust bracket

Rear shock absorber

Axle leaf spring u-clamp

A touch of mink
The reclining, leather-covered seats were plushly upholstered and very comfortable. Before a Cadillac was sent to the showroom, the upholstery was rubbed all over with pieces of m... if the fur caught, or was the slightest bit worn when the rubbing stopped, the car had failed "the mink test" and was reupholstered.

AUSTIN MINI

IN 1957, ALEX ISSIGONIS, head designer at the British Motor Corporation, was asked by the BMC to design the smallest possible car capable of carrying four people. Two years later, the Mini was unveiled. At first, few people took the car seriously. But when it became obvious that the Mini was roomy, efficient, and cheap to run, sales soared. In 1986, the five-millionth Mini rolled off the production line.

Wheels

A small car needs small wheels. Large ones would have required wheel arches that used up too much passenger space. Issigonis decided to use ten-inch (25.4-cm) wheels with a wheel rim of about three inches (8.9 cm). No company had ever produced tires of this size. Happily, one tire company, Dunlop, agreed to develop them.

The Mini Cooper

In 1961, BMC built the Mini Cooper, a version with a 997 cc engine. It was a huge success at racing circuits and rallies. In 1965, Paddy Hopkirk and Henry Liddon won the Monte Carlo Rally, a race across Europe, in a Cooper. During a hair-raising journey, they lost their way, came into the gunsights of a Russian soldier, and were stopped by French police.

The engine

The prototype Mini, affectionately known as "The Orange Box," was fitted with a 948 cc engine. This gave it a top speed of 85 mph (136 km/h).

Roof panel

Rear quarter window

Driver's seat

Front seat adjustor

Spare tire and wheel

Trunk panel

Driver's door

Rear wheel arch

Rear panel

Main chassis

Front tire

Front wheel

Front hubcap

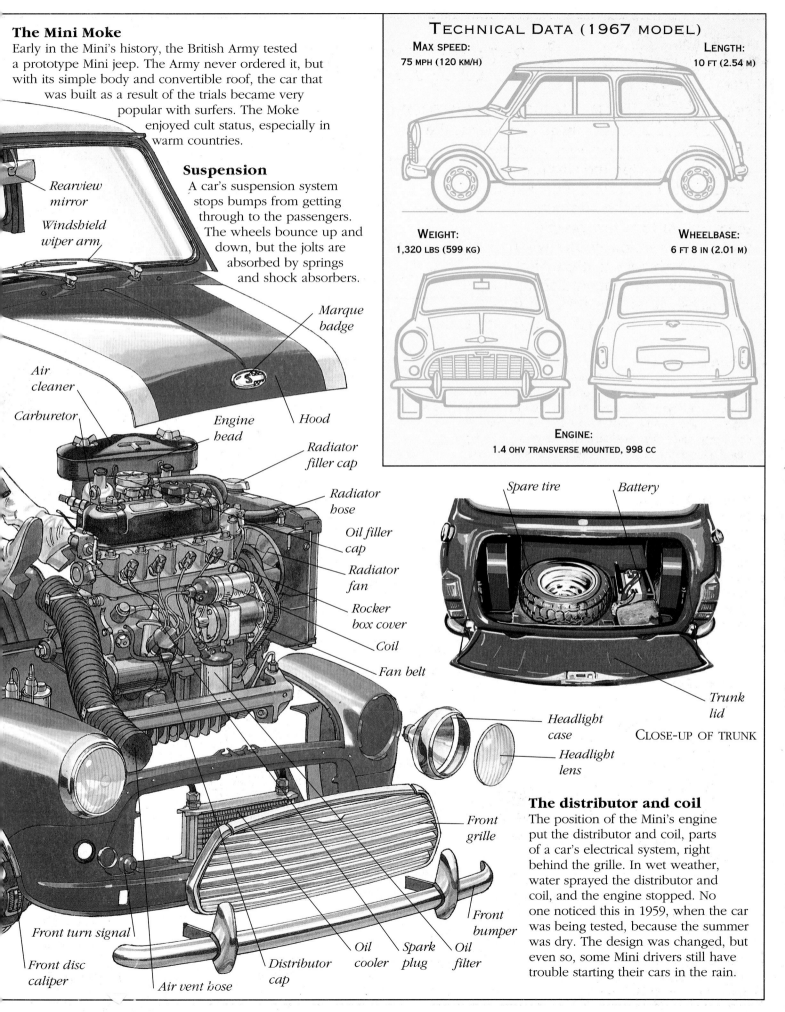

The Mini Moke

Early in the Mini's history, the British Army tested a prototype Mini jeep. The Army never ordered it, but with its simple body and convertible roof, the car that was built as a result of the trials became very popular with surfers. The Moke enjoyed cult status, especially in warm countries.

Suspension

A car's suspension system stops bumps from getting through to the passengers. The wheels bounce up and down, but the jolts are absorbed by springs and shock absorbers.

Rearview mirror

Windshield wiper arm

Air cleaner

Carburetor

Marque badge

Engine head

Hood

Radiator filler cap

Radiator hose

Oil filler cap

Radiator fan

Rocker box cover

Coil

Fan belt

Front grille

Front bumper

Front turn signal

Front disc caliper

Air vent hose

Distributor cap

Oil cooler

Spark plug

Oil filter

TECHNICAL DATA (1967 MODEL)

MAX SPEED:
75 MPH (120 KM/H)

LENGTH:
10 FT (2.54 M)

WEIGHT:
1,320 LBS (599 KG)

WHEELBASE:
6 FT 8 IN (2.01 M)

ENGINE:
1.4 OHV TRANSVERSE MOUNTED, 998 CC

Spare tire

Battery

Trunk lid

CLOSE-UP OF TRUNK

Headlight case

Headlight lens

The distributor and coil

The position of the Mini's engine put the distributor and coil, parts of a car's electrical system, right behind the grille. In wet weather, water sprayed the distributor and coil, and the engine stopped. No one noticed this in 1959, when the car was being tested, because the summer was dry. The design was changed, but even so, some Mini drivers still have trouble starting their cars in the rain.

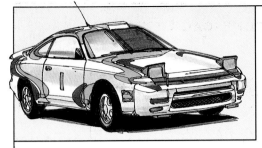

RALLY CAR

RALLY DRIVING IS PROBABLY the roughest and toughest of all competition driving. The cars must be able to run along mountain tracks, drive across deserts, blast through blizzards, ride across rivers, and screech around narrow streets at breakneck speeds. They must be as efficient in Arctic conditions as they are in tropical sandstorms. To be eligible for rally races, at least 5000 identical models of each competition car must be made. Among the many companies that have entered the rally game is the Japanese carmaker Toyota.

Headlight lens

Pop-up headlight housing

Front protective mesh

Air cleaning housing

Air box intake hose

Four-wheel power

Distributor

In most cars, power is transmitted from the engine to either the front wheels or the back wheels. In the Toyota, and most other modern rally cars, the transmission system takes power to all four wheels. This helps the cars cope with the stress of being driven at full speed over a wide range of surfaces.

Cooling fan housing

Cooling fan

Retaining bracket

Front driveshaft

Front shock absorber spring

The safari

The Toyota team has had its greatest success in the Safari Rally, held in Kenya every year. Conditions are so tough that drivers can sometimes fall days behind schedule. Tropical storms can reduce dusty roads to deep mudbaths within minutes, and turn fordable streams into raging torrents, leaving rally cars and support vehicles marooned for days.

Front disc brake

Windshield wiper arm

Fluid reservoir

Clutch pedal

Front tire (cross section)

Front wheel retaining nut

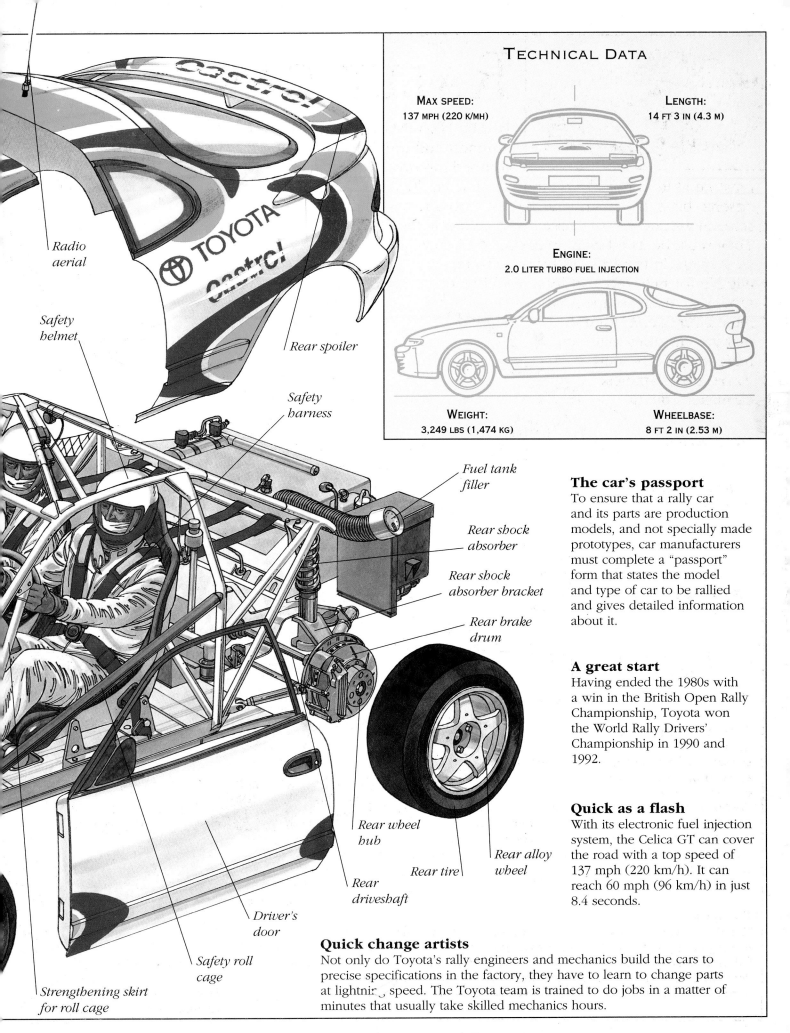

Radio
aerial

Safety
helmet

Rear spoiler

Safety
harness

TECHNICAL DATA

MAX SPEED:		LENGTH:
137 MPH (220 K/MH)		14 FT 3 IN (4.3 M)

ENGINE:
2.0 LITER TURBO FUEL INJECTION

WEIGHT:		WHEELBASE:
3,249 LBS (1,474 KG)		8 FT 2 IN (2.53 M)

Fuel tank
filler

Rear shock
absorber

Rear shock
absorber bracket

Rear brake
drum

Rear wheel
hub

Rear alloy
wheel

Rear tire

Rear
driveshaft

Driver's
door

Safety roll
cage

Strengthening skirt
for roll cage

The car's passport

To ensure that a rally car
and its parts are production
models, and not specially made
prototypes, car manufacturers
must complete a "passport"
form that states the model
and type of car to be rallied
and gives detailed information
about it.

A great start

Having ended the 1980s with
a win in the British Open Rally
Championship, Toyota won
the World Rally Drivers'
Championship in 1990 and
1992.

Quick as a flash

With its electronic fuel injection
system, the Celica GT can cover
the road with a top speed of
137 mph (220 km/h). It can
reach 60 mph (96 km/h) in just
8.4 seconds.

Quick change artists

Not only do Toyota's rally engineers and mechanics build the cars to
precise specifications in the factory, they have to learn to change parts
at lightning speed. The Toyota team is trained to do jobs in a matter of
minutes that usually take skilled mechanics hours.

FERRARI

IN 11.2 SECONDS A FERRARI *TESTAROSSA* can go from 0 to 100 mph (160 km/h). A few seconds later, it can reach its official top speed of 181 mph (289.6 km/h) – well over 2.5 times the speed limit in most countries in the world! The speedometer reads up to 200 mph (320 km/h). The *Testa Rossi* (Red Head) was one of the most successful race cars of the 1960s and 1970s, so when Ferrari produced a top of the range road car, they decided to recall their days of glory on the racing circuit. In October 1984, a vivid red *Testarossa* drew gasps of admiration at the Paris Motor Show. In mid-1985 a new *Testarossa* cost well over $90,000. By 1994 the price had almost doubled, and with production limited to 4,000 a year, there is a waiting list of up to three years.

FERRARI LOGO
ON HUBCAP

Star car
Perhaps the most famous *Testarossa* is the white one that starred in the TV series *Miami Vice*. When filming started, the makers used replicas. Ferrari took the makers to court, and soon the stars were behind the wheel of the real thing!

High-speed gears
The *Testarossa* has five-speed gears. In first gear it has a maximum speed of 50.4 mph (80.6 km/h). That means it can go as fast in first gear as many cars go in top gear. The other gear speeds are just as impressive.

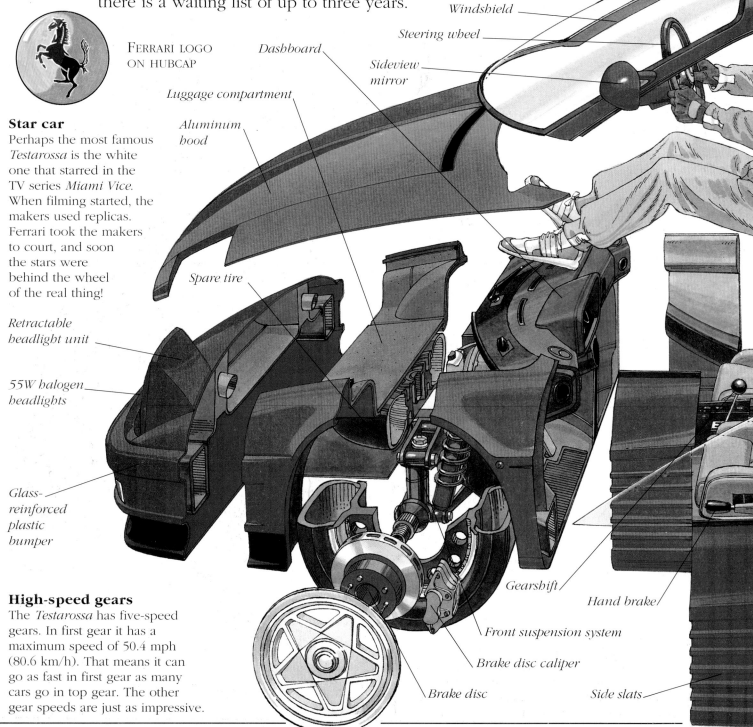

Windshield

Steering wheel

Sideview mirror

Dashboard

Luggage compartment

Aluminum hood

Spare tire

Retractable headlight unit

55W halogen headlights

Glass-reinforced plastic bumper

Gearshift

Hand brake

Front suspension system

Brake disc caliper

Brake disc

Side slats

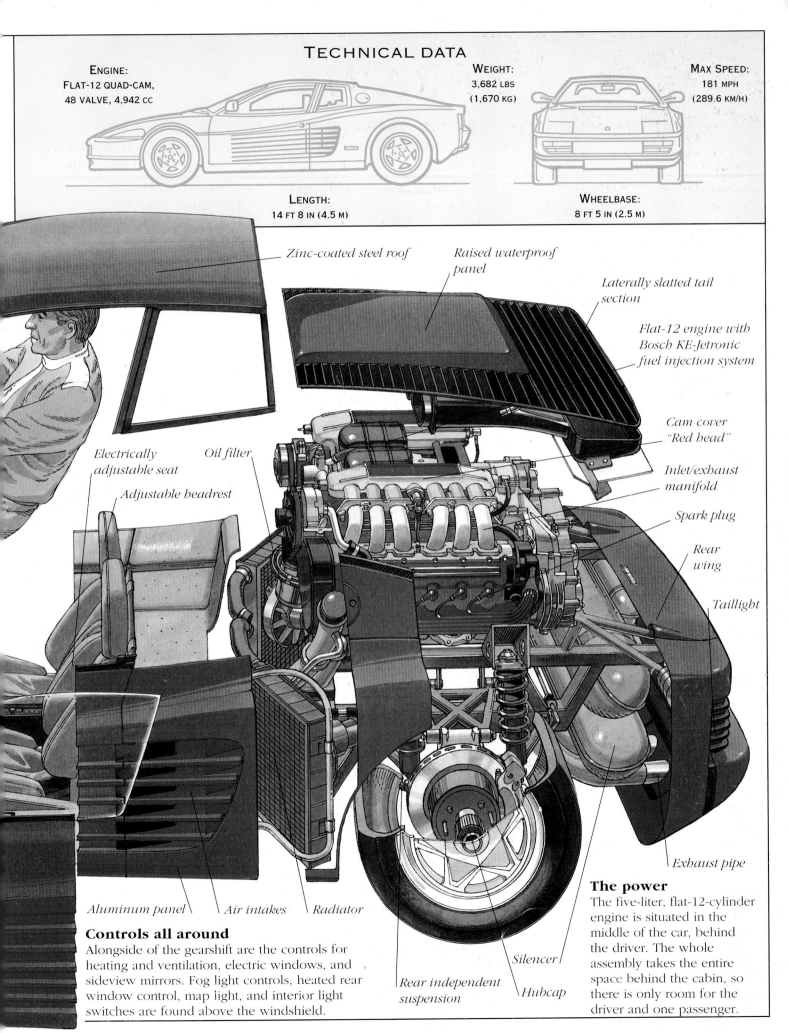

TECHNICAL DATA

ENGINE:	WEIGHT:	MAX SPEED:
FLAT-12 QUAD-CAM, 48 VALVE, 4,942 cc	3,682 LBS (1,670 KG)	181 MPH (289.6 KM/H)

LENGTH:
14 FT 8 IN (4.5 M)

WHEELBASE:
8 FT 5 IN (2.5 M)

Zinc-coated steel roof

Raised waterproof panel

Laterally slatted tail section

Flat-12 engine with Bosch KE-Jetronic fuel injection system

Cam cover "Red head"

Inlet/exhaust manifold

Spark plug

Rear wing

Taillight

Electrically adjustable seat

Oil filter

Adjustable headrest

Aluminum panel

Air intakes

Radiator

Exhaust pipe

Silencer

Rear independent suspension

Hubcap

Controls all around

Alongside of the gearshift are the controls for heating and ventilation, electric windows, and sideview mirrors. Fog light controls, heated rear window control, map light, and interior light switches are found above the windshield.

The power

The five-liter, flat-12-cylinder engine is situated in the middle of the car, behind the driver. The whole assembly takes the entire space behind the cabin, so there is only room for the driver and one passenger.

FORMULA I

WHAT COULD THE LABEL STITCHED INTO THE BACK of a sweater have in common with a car roaring around a Grand Prix racetrack? They both bear the name Benetton! The Italian knitwear company first came into Grand Prix racing in 1983 when they started to sponsor the Tyrrell team, which was renamed Benetton-Tyrrell. In 1986, they went into Formula I racing in their own right with a car powered by a BMW engine, later replaced with one designed by Ford in association with Cosworth Engineering. In 1988, Grand Prixs were dominated by McLaren-Honda, but Benetton placed in 12 of the season's 16 races. A major force had arrived in the world of motor racing.

Fastest lap
The 1988 Benetton-Ford clocked up the fastest lap in the German Grand Prix at the Hockenheim Circuit. With Alessandro Naninni at the wheel, the car ate up the 5.2-mile (8.3-km) circuit in 2.49 minutes. That's an average of 124.3 mph (200 km/h).

Real smoothies
If the track is dry, Grand Prix cars are fitted with treadless tires. This allows a large area of the tire to be on the track and makes the car more stable. Tires with treads are used if it is wet. These give the car a better grip.

Made in Britain
Benetton-Fords are made in a factory near the village of Enstone in Oxfordshire. The workshop looks more like an operating theater than a car factory, with skilled technicians clad in white overalls and safety caps working with the same precision as top surgeons. Building race cars is expensive. The factory cost $18 million to set up.

On the wing
Formula I cars are fitted with two sets of wings, or airfoils, one low down at the front and another at the back. The car travels so fast that without these, it could lift up off the track like an airplane. The airfoils are designed so that the air rushes over them and pushes the car down to hold it onto the track.

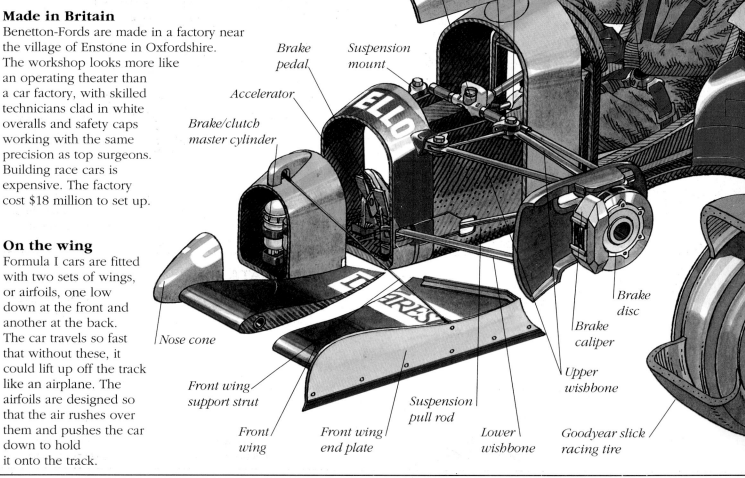
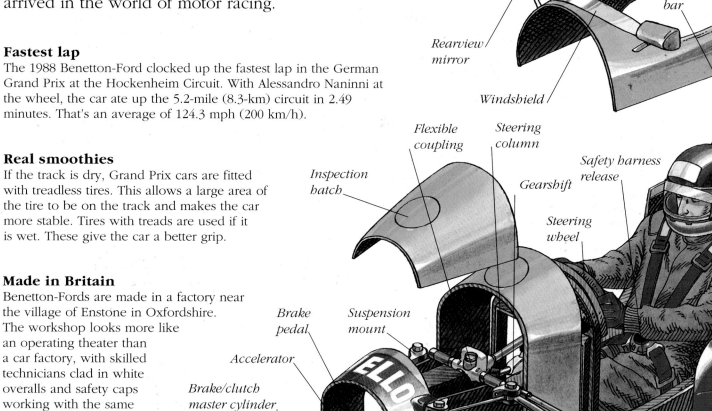

Rollover bar

Rearview mirror

Windshield

Flexible coupling

Steering column

Safety harness release

Inspection hatch

Gearshift

Steering wheel

Brake pedal

Suspension mount

Accelerator

Brake/clutch master cylinder

Nose cone

Brake disc

Brake caliper

Front wing support strut

Front wing

Front wing end plate

Suspension pull rod

Lower wishbone

Upper wishbone

Goodyear slick racing tire

Air intake

Engine cowling

Ford Cosworth engine

Fuel injection air-intake trumpet

Cam cover

Spark plug

Rear wing

Exhaust pipe leader

Well timed

Formula I cars are fitted with small radio transmitters. Each of them operates on its own frequency. Throughout the race, they send out impulses that are received by trackside computers. The computers recognize the cars' signals and calculate the speed the cars are traveling at to within a fraction of a second. This information is relayed throughout the race to the press and the crews in the pits.

Inspection hatch

Fuel tank

20

The pits

Teams have their own workshops at the side of the racetrack, called pits. During a race, cars stop in the pits to refuel, to have worn-out parts replaced, and to have wheels changed. Time is so vital that the mechanics are trained to work at lightning speed.

Hub

Quick-release center lock wheel

Exhaust tailpipe

Radiator

Onboard electronics

Radiator grille

Wheel bolt

Wheel rim

Waving the flag

Race officials use flags to send messages to drivers. A red flag tells them to stop racing immediately. A yellow one warns of danger and a green one means that the hazard has been removed. Black with an orange circle warns the driver whose number is shown that there is something wrong with the car. Finally, a checkered flag is waved when the race is over.

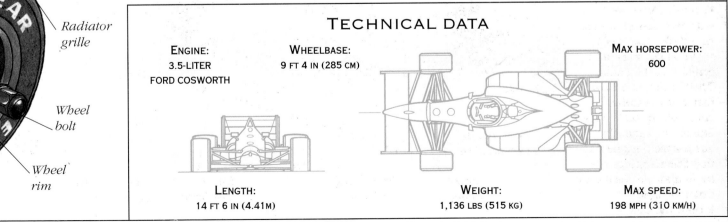

TECHNICAL DATA

ENGINE:	WHEELBASE:		MAX HORSEPOWER:
3.5-LITER FORD COSWORTH	9 FT 4 IN (285 CM)		600

LENGTH:	WEIGHT:	MAX SPEED:
14 FT 6 IN (4.41M)	1,136 LBS (515 KG)	198 MPH (310 KM/H)

CAR TIMELINE

THE STORY OF THE THE CAR BEGAN only slightly more than 100 years ago. Since that time, the automobile has evolved from a horse-drawn carriage look-alike to an aerodynamic, fuel-efficient, and powerful machine. Along the way, the car's basic design has acquired many innovations, such as supercharging, monocoque construction, and front-wheel drive. With exploration into electric- and solar-powered transportation, future innovations may entirely transform the automobile yet again.

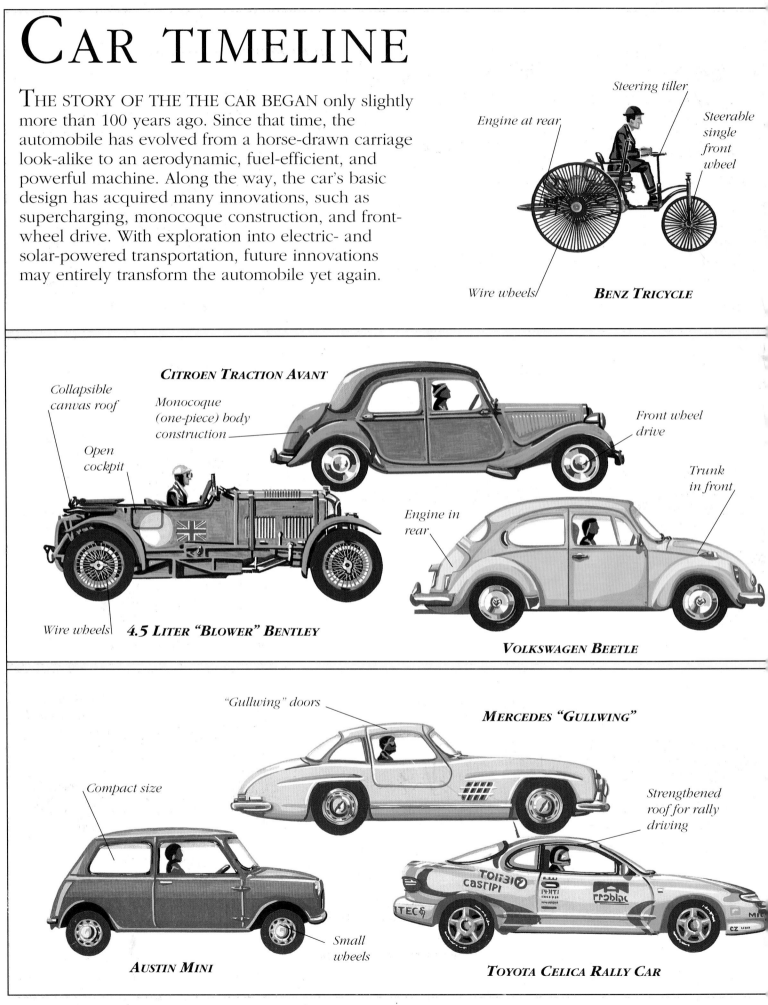

Steering tiller

Engine at rear

Steerable single front wheel

Wire wheels

BENZ TRICYCLE

Collapsible canvas roof

CITROEN TRACTION AVANT

Monocoque (one-piece) body construction

Open cockpit

Front wheel drive

Trunk in front

Engine in rear

Wire wheels   **4.5 LITER "BLOWER" BENTLEY**

VOLKSWAGEN BEETLE

"Gullwing" doors

MERCEDES "GULLWING"

Compact size

Strengthened roof for rally driving

Small wheels

AUSTIN MINI

TOYOTA CELICA RALLY CAR

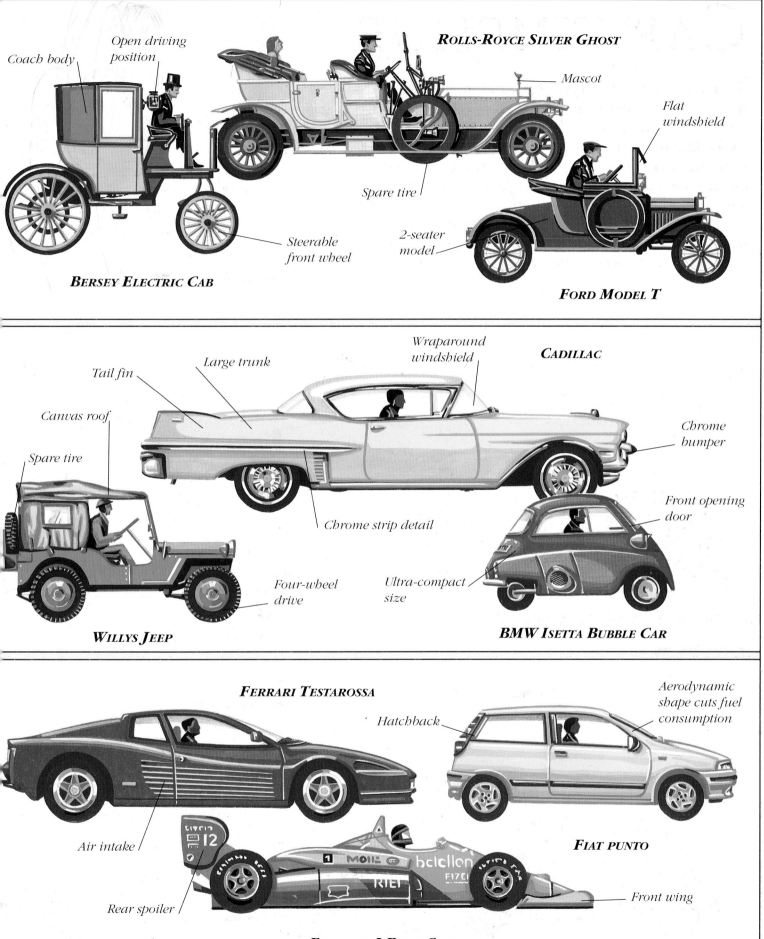

Coach body

Open driving position

ROLLS-ROYCE SILVER GHOST

Mascot

Flat windshield

Spare tire

Steerable front wheel

2-seater model

BERSEY ELECTRIC CAB

FORD MODEL T

Wraparound windshield

CADILLAC

Large trunk

Tail fin

Canvas roof

Chrome bumper

Spare tire

Front opening door

Chrome strip detail

Four-wheel drive

Ultra-compact size

WILLYS JEEP

BMW ISETTA BUBBLE CAR

FERRARI TESTAROSSA

Aerodynamic shape cuts fuel consumption

Hatchback

Air intake

Rear spoiler

Front wing

FIAT PUNTO

FORMULA I RACE CAR

GLOSSARY

Accelerator pump
A device fitted to the carburetor to provide extra fuel to the fuel/air mixture when the accelerator pedal is pressed down.

Air cooling
A way of cooling the engine using an engine-driven fan that forces cool air over the engine's surfaces at high speeds.

Alternator
A device for turning rotating mechanical energy into electrical energy.

Ammeter
A device that measures the electrical current supplied to the battery by the alternator or drawn from the battery by the car's electrical system.

Antifreeze
A chemical added to the water in the cooling system to reduce the temperature at which it freezes.

Automatic transmission
A gearbox that selects the correct gear ratio when the car is moving according to the car's speed and load.

Axle
The spindle on which a wheel revolves.

Battery
The part of the car that supplies the power that works the lights, ignition, radio, and other parts of the car that function by electricity.

Bearing
A hard-wearing surface, usually metal, designed to cut down wear and friction when it moves another part.

Big end
The end of the connecting rod, attached to the crankshaft, that transmits the rod's movement to the crankshaft.

Brake caliper
Part of a disc brake housing the brake pads and hydraulic pistons.

Brake disc
The rotating disc part of a disc brake system, clamped between friction pads.

Brake horsepower (BHP)
A measure of the power needed to bring a moving body to a halt.

Brake pad
The friction material and metal backing-plate of a disc brake system.

Brake shoe
The friction material and the curved metal part of a drum brake system.

Brakes
The discs or drums that bring the car to a halt when they are put into contact with the wheels.

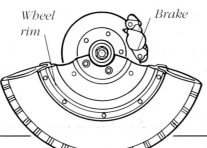

Wheel rim   Brake

Camshaft
The shaft driven by the crankshaft that operates the engine's valves.

Carburetor
The device that sprays a mixture of gasoline and air into the cylinders.

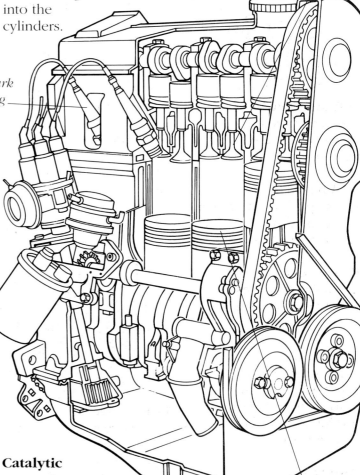

Spark plug

Valve

Piston

Catalytic converter
Part of the exhaust system that cuts down the amount of harmful gases released into the air.

Chassis
The rigid frame on which the car's body is built.

Choke
A device, used in cold weather when starting a car, that reduces the amount of air in the carburetor. This makes the fuel/air mixture easier to ignite.

Clutch
The pedal that, when pressed, disconnects the engine from the gearbox to enable the driver to change gear.

Combustion chamber
The part of the cylinder head where the fuel/air mixture is compressed by a piston and ignited by a spark.

Crankcase
The part of the cylinder block that houses the crankshaft.

Cylinder
The metal tube encasing a sliding piston.

Cylinder block
The part of the engine that contains the cylinders, crankshaft, and pistons.

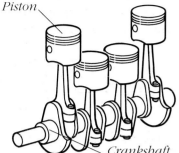

Piston

Crankshaft

Cylinder head
The part at the top of an engine where the valves are situated.

Dashboard
The strip of wood or metal facing the driver on which the instruments are fitted.

Diesel engine
An engine that runs on diesel oil rather than refined gasoline.

Differential
The system of gears in the transmission system that enables the wheels to turn at different speeds when turning corners.

Disc brake
A brake with a rotating disc held by clamps between hydraulically operated friction pads.

Drum brake
A braking system whereby "shoes," lined with friction pads, run inside a cylindrical drum attached to the wheel.

Exhaust pipe
The metal tube along which fumes run from the engine to be expelled into the air.

Filter
A device for removing unwanted particles from air, oil, or fuel.

Fuel injection
A way of introducing fuel into the engine that increases performance.

Gear lever
The column that the driver moves after operating the clutch to change gear.

Gearbox
The part of the transmission system that provides the different gears that enable the car to be driven at different speeds.

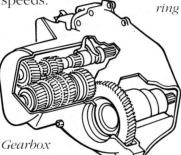

Gearbox

Horsepower
A measurement of power.

Hydraulics
The transmission of pressure through a fluid.

Independent suspension
A suspension system by which the movement of one wheel of a pair has no effect on the other.

Ignition system
The electrical system, made up of the battery, ignition coil, distributor, switch, spark plugs, and wiring, that provides the spark that ignites the air/fuel mixture in the engine.

Leaded gasoline
Gasoline with extra lead added to it during manufacturing.

Piston
The metal part that fits tightly inside a cylinder and slides up and down to turn the crankshaft.

Piston ring
A strong metal ring that runs around a piston to ensure the tightest possible seal between the piston and the cylinder wall.

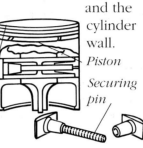

Piston

Securing pin

Piston ring

Power steering
A system that uses hydraulic fluid pressure, supplied by an engine-driven pump, to make the steering system more responsive to the touch.

Quarter light
The small triangular window fitted in front of the front side window and behind the rear one.

Shock absorber
The part that cushions or dampens the bumps that happen when a car is driven over an uneven surface.

Spark ignition
The system whereby a spark, produced by the spark plugs, ignites the fuel/air mixture drawn into the engine cylinders, thus providing the power to drive the engine.

Spark plug
The pair of electrodes, separated by a ceramic surface, that produce the spark in the spark ignition system.

Spark plug

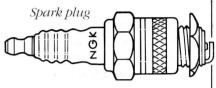

Suspension
The parts of the car that hold it over the wheels.

Synchromesh
Part of the gearbox that matches the speed of one gear with another to ensure smooth gear changes.

Tachometer
A device that measures the speed of the engine in revolutions per minute. Also known as the "rev counter."

Torque
The turning force generated by a rotating part.

Unleaded gasoline
Gasoline that has a natural lead content with none added in manufacturing.

Valve
A device that opens to allow gas or fluid to flow through it, and closes to stop the flow.

Vee engine
An engine in which the cylinders are fitted in two banks that form a V-shape.

INDEX

A

airfoils, 26
ammeter, 7
assembly line, 6
Austin Mini, 20-21
autronic eye, 19

B

Bantam Car Corporation, 13
Beetle, 14-15
Bennetton-Ford, 26
Bennetton-Tyrrell, 26
Bentley Blower, 8-9
Bentley, Walter O., 9
Birkin, Sir Henry "Tim," 8
British Motor Corporation (BMC), 20

C

Cadillac Sedan de Ville, 18-19
Carrera Panamericana, Mexico, 16
Celica GT, 22-23
chassis, 8
Citroën, André, 10
Citroën "A" Series
        7CV, 10-11
        11CV, 11
coachwork, 8
combustion chambers, 17
Cosworth Engineering, 26
Coupe de Ville, 19
cranking, 6
cylinders, 8, 14, 17

D

dashboard
        in Bentley Blower, 9
        in Model T Ford, 7
distributor and coil, in Austin Mini, 21
Dunlop, 20

E

engine, 8
        in Austin Mini, 20 21
        in Citroën, 11
        in Ferrari *Testarossa*, 25
        in Formula I car, 26
        in Model T Ford, 6
        in Volkswagen Beetle, 14
exhaust, 11

F

Ferrari *Testarossa*, 24-25
five-speed gears, in Ferrari, 24
flags, in Formula I racing, 27
Ford,
        Model A, 6
        Model T, 6-7
Ford, Henry, 13
Ford Motor Company, 6, 13
Formula I race car, 26-27
four-wheel drive, 12, 22
front-wheel drive, 10
fuel injection, 17, 23

G

gears,
        Model T Ford, 7
        Volkswagen, 15
Goodyear, 26
Grand Prix racing, 26
Gullwing, 16-17
gullwing doors, 16

I

Issigonis, Alex, 20

J

Jeep, 12-13

L

Le Mans, 9, 16

M

Mercedes-Benz 300SL, 16-17
Mille Miglia road race, 16
Mini, 20-21
        Cooper, 20
        Moke, 21
Model A Ford, 6
Model T Ford, 6-7
Monte Carlo Rally, 20

N

Naninni, Alessandro, 26

P

pits, 27
Porsche, Ferdinand, 14
power steering, 18

R

race car,
        Bennetton-Ford, 26-27
        Gullwing, 16-17
radio transmitter, in Formula I cars, 27
rally car, 22-23

S

Safari Rally, 22
Sedan de Ville, 18-19

SL (Sports Light), 16
speed, of Ferrari, 24
starting handle, 6
supercharger, 8, 9
suspension, 10, 20
synchromeshing, 15

T

tachometer, 9
tail fins, 18
Testarossa, 24-25
tin lizzies, 6
torque, 11
torsion bar, 10
Toyota Celica GT, 22-23
Traction Avant, 10, 11
transmission, 11, 22
trunk, in Sedan de Ville, 18-19
tires, for Formula I cars, 26

U

upholstery, in Sedan de Ville, 19

V

Villiers, Amherst, 8
Volkswagen, 14-15

W

welding, automatic, 15
wheels, on Austin Mini, 20
Willys Jeep, 12-13
Willys Overland Motors Inc., 13

Acknowledgments

Dorling Kindersley would like to thank the following people who helped in the preparation of this book:
Lynn Bresler for the index
Additional artworks by John See